IF FOUND

👤 _____

✉ _____

📱 _____

Greater Than a Tourist Book Series
Reviews from Readers

I think the series is wonderful and beneficial for tourists to get information before visiting the city.

-Seckin Zumbul, Izmir Turkey

I am a world traveler who has read many trip guides but this one really made a difference for me. I would call it a heartfelt creation of a local guide expert instead of just a guide.

-Susy, Isla Holbox, Mexico

New to the area like me, this is a must have!

-Joe, Bloomington, USA

This is a good series that gets down to it when looking for things to do at your destination without having to read a novel for just a few ideas.

-Rachel, Monterey, USA

Good information to have to plan my trip to this destination.

-Pennie Farrell, Mexico

Great ideas for a port day.

-Mary Martin USA

Aptly titled, you won't just be a tourist after reading this book. You'll be greater than a tourist!

-Alan Warner, Grand Rapids, USA

Even though I only have three days to spend in San Miguel in an upcoming visit, I will use the author's suggestions to guide some of my time there. An easy read - with chapters named to guide me in directions I want to go.

 -Robert Catapano, USA

Great insights from a local perspective! Useful information and a very good value!

 -Sarah, USA

This series provides an in-depth experience through the eyes of a local. Reading these series will help you to travel the city in with confidence and it'll make your journey a unique one.

-Andrew Teoh, Ipoh, Malaysia

>TOURIST

GREATER THAN A TOURIST- PENSACOLA FLORIDA USA

50 Travel Tips from a Local

Mary Rosado

Greater Than a Tourist - Pensacola, Florida, U.S.A Copyright © 2019 by CZYK Publishing LLC. All Rights Reserved.

All rights reserved. No part of this book may be reproduced in any form or by any electronic or mechanical means including information storage and retrieval systems, without permission in writing from the author. The only exception is by a reviewer, who may quote short excerpts in a review.

The statements in this book are of the authors and may not be the views of CZYK Publishing or Greater Than a Tourist.

Cover designed by: Ivana Stamenkovic
Cover Image:

CZYK Publishing Since 2011.

Greater Than a Tourist
Visit our website at www.GreaterThanaTourist.com

Lock Haven, PA
All rights reserved.
ISBN: 9781793123190

>TOURIST
50 TRAVEL TIPS FROM A LOCAL

>TOURIST

BOOK DESCRIPTION

Are you excited about planning your next trip? Do you want to try something new? Would you like some guidance from a local? If you answered yes to any of these questions, then this Greater Than a Tourist book is for you.

Greater Than a Tourist - Pensacola, Florida, U.S.A., by Mary Rosado, offers the inside scoop on the Pensacola area.

We all have different expectations when traveling. This book offers a collection of this author's insights and recommendations of new places, travel approaches, and experiences. The content is intended to serve as suggestions for your visit; the end result is yours to sculpt. As you travel, people are the best sources of tips and information. Their information is fresh, honest, and up-to-date.

Safe travels and may your experience be Greater Than a Tourist! Most travel books tell you how to travel like a tourist. Although there is nothing wrong with that, as part of the Greater Than a Tourist series, this book will give you travel tips from someone who has lived at your next travel destination.

In these pages, you will discover advice that will help you throughout your stay. This book will not tell you exact addresses or store hours but instead will give you excitement and knowledge from a local that you may not find in other smaller print travel books

Travel like a local. Slow down, stay in one place, and get to know the people and the culture. By the time you finish this book, you will be eager and prepared to travel to your next destination.

>TOURIST

TABLE OF CONTENTS

BOOK DESCRIPTION
TABLE OF CONTENTS
DEDICATION
ABOUT THE AUTHOR
HOW TO USE THIS BOOK
FROM THE PUBLISHER
OUR STORY
WELCOME TO
> TOURIST
1. The Beach is Why You Came Here
2. Crowds or Quiet on Your Beach?
3. Where to Stay
4. Get to the Pier
5. I Want to Go Fishing but I Don't Have a Boat
6. Joe Patti's: More Than Just a Fish Market
7. Snorkeling
8. Entering the Pensacola Naval Air Station
9. A Lighthouse with More Than Just a View
10. See a Blue Angel Practice from the Top of the Lighthouse
11. Peg Leg Pete's is Worth the Wait
12. If You Love Baseball
13. Best of the Best Bushwhacker
14. Fort Pickens is a Must

15. Hot, Sandy Music
16. Incredible Scuba Diving
17. Downtown Night Life
18. You've Got to Try a Dueling Piano Bar
19. Be the Scene
20. Frisky Dolphin for the Best Oysters
21. The De Luna Winery
22. Proper Footwear
23. Beach Toys – BYO or You Can Rent
24. Head East on Santa Rosa Island
25. Navarre Beach
26. Pensacola NAS Museum
27. If You've Never Seen an Airshow
28. These Pelicans Won't Fly Away
29. Shopping on Palafox
30. Jaco's for Dining Deluxe
31. Watersports Rentals
32. A Dolphin Cruise is Worth the Money
33. Ghost Hunting in Pensacola
34. Pensacola Historical Tidbits
35. Great Greek Flavors to Go
36. Pensacon
37. Sounds Interesting… Maybe I'll Drive By
38. Historic Pensacola
39. Wall South Vietnam Memorial
40. A Hardware Store That's Not All Hardware

>TOURIST

41. You'll Go Nuts at the Renfroe Pecan Company
42. Pizza Pizza
43. You're Close to L.A.
44. #1 Beach Bar in the U.S.A.
45. Know Your Beach Flags and Rip Currents
46. An Irish, Irish Pub
47. A Flounder Dining Adventure
48. River Options
49. The Old Hickory Whiskey Bar
50. Bocce Ball Makes Friends

TOP REASONS TO BOOK THIS TRIP
50 THINGS TO KNOW ABOUT PACKING LIGHT FOR TRAVEL
Packing and Planning Tips
Travel Questions
Travel Bucket List
NOTES

DEDICATION

This book is dedicated to my husband. As we travel along in life's pickup truck (because it's a bumpy road), sometimes he's the driver and sometimes I am. Together, we always make it to the next destination.

ABOUT THE AUTHOR

Mary Rosado is a freelance writer and street photographer living in Pensacola, FL. After coming to the area as a tourist, it was destined to be her next home. Mary focuses her photography and writing on capturing overlooked details and new perspectives to bring events and images to life. Along with her creative writing, she provides ghost writing and resume writing services.

Mary's numerous relocations (37 to date, in North and South America) have inspired a lifestyle of perpetual exploration and embracing new missions. She welcomes the challenge of the next journey to provide fresh subjects and new ideas for her writing and photography.

\>TOURIST

HOW TO USE THIS BOOK

The Greater Than a Tourist book series was written by someone who has lived in an area for over three months. The goal of this book is to help travelers either dream or experience different locations by providing opinions from a local. The author has made suggestions based on their own experiences. Please do your own research before traveling to the area in case the suggested places are unavailable.

Travel Advisories: As a first step in planning any trip abroad, check the Travel Advisories for your intended destination.
https://travel.state.gov/content/travel/en/traveladvisories/traveladvisories.html

FROM THE PUBLISHER

Traveling can be one of the most important parts of a person's life. The anticipation and memories that you have are some of the best. As a publisher of the Greater Than a Tourist book series, as well as the popular 50 Things to Know book series, we strive to help you learn about new places, spark your imagination, and inspire you. Wherever you are and whatever you do I wish you safe, fun, and inspiring travel.

Lisa Rusczyk Ed. D.
CZYK Publishing

OUR STORY

Traveling is a passion of the "Greater than a Tourist" series creator. Lisa studied abroad in college, and for their honeymoon Lisa and her husband toured Europe. During her travels to Malta, an older man tried to give her some advice based on his own experience living on the island since he was a young boy. She was not sure if she should talk to the stranger but was interested in his advice. When traveling to some places she was wary to talk to locals because she was afraid that they weren't being genuine. Through her travels, Lisa learned how much locals had to share with tourists. Lisa created the "Greater Than a Tourist" book series to help connect people with locals. A topic that locals are very passionate about sharing.

>TOURIST

WELCOME TO
> TOURIST

>TOURIST

Your next destination is the best one yet. Hope and the promise of new experiences are the charging stations of life.

~ Mary Rosado

1. THE BEACH IS WHY YOU CAME HERE

Everyone loves the beach; it's the go-to place to relax the mind and revitalize the soul. Surf and sand can transport us to a better place, even if just for the day. The sugar white sand and emerald green water of Pensacola beaches deliver on that promise.

Pensacola has an assortment of beach-crowd types. The heart of Pensacola Beach is teeming with suntanned bodies, lively music, and non-stop action. It's THE scene. Beyond the main beach, the pace slows slightly and sandcastles, inflatable ducks, and boogie boards populate the sands. More remote areas offer unobstructed views of the surf and a quieter beach experience. No matter which beach you head to, the Pensacola sand will squeak beneath your feet; the noise is said to be a reminder to focus on the beach instead of your troubles.

Choose your beach. The white sands and blue-green waters will deliver whatever you're looking for and it's all right here in Pensacolahhhh.

2. CROWDS OR QUIET ON YOUR BEACH?

Whether you're coming from the east, the west, or the north, once you get to Pensacola, the route to the beach is the same for all. The beach is on an island and most will cross two bridges to get there.

After crossing the second bridge to Pensacola Beach (there's a $1.00 toll and at times, significant bridge-backup), the iconic Beach Ball Tower is almost straight ahead. The Gulf of Mexico is in front of you and the Santa Rosa Sound is the water behind you. Knowing your mission for your beach day will help determine your direction from here. Do I want crowds or a quieter setting?

The base of the Beach Ball is Casino Beach. Crowd lovers will want to park here; this beach is the action-packed, body-watching destination. Unpack

>TOURIST

your beach towels, mark your spot, and take in the excitement of the scene in front of you.

If you head further east or west away from the Beach Ball Tower, the people density diminishes. There are multiple parking locations as you proceed; the only problem will be hauling a full day's worth of umbrellas, blankets, and food to your spot because that's how long you'll want to stay. The sand, the sun, and the crystal blue will return you to your inner-kid self.

3. WHERE TO STAY

If you're unfamiliar with the geography of the area, Pensacola and Pensacola Beach are in two different zip codes. Pensacola Beach sits on Santa Rosa Island and is truly a beach town, while Pensacola is on the mainland. Inland Pensacola offers more cultural aspects of the two locations.

To get to Pensacola Beach from Pensacola, you will cross two bridges, passing through the City of Gulf Breeze on the peninsula of land that sits between them. Remember that from the beach area, Gulf Breeze is the closest option for groceries, medical care, and most of your vacation staple items.

Downtown Pensacola Beach offers dozens of hotel options from major U.S. hotel chains to small bed & breakfast options. You'll find rooms facing the Gulf of Mexico, downtown, or the Sound. There are hi-rise, mid-rise, and low-rise options; prices vary from uber-expensive to modest. Your budget and their space availability will narrow down your choices. If you're looking for a beach house or condo, there are hundreds available through the online residential rental sites.

The mainland city of Pensacola also has both hotel and residential rental options. For the most part, places to stay on the mainland are not waterfront as the actual beach is across the bridges, nine miles away. It's not a huge city (population 52,000 plus) so navigating the streets and highways is not difficult. If you plan to stay on the mainland and don't want to drive to the beach, there is a passenger ferry operating from downtown to two areas on the island although transport times are limited (the future of the ferry operations is pending at the time of this publication). Otherwise, head south over the bridges and keep in mind the traffic and toll on the Pensacola Bridge may slow you down.

>TOURIST

4. GET TO THE PIER

The Pensacola Beach Gulf Pier offers more than a quarter mile of incredible panoramic views, superior fishing, and above-average people watching. From extraordinary marine life to unbelievable sunsets, if you don't find something here to catch your eye, you're just not looking. Yes, it's a popular tourist destination but there is nowhere else in Pensacola to get the unobstructed views of the vast beauty of the Gulf. Stop, stand, and look… most of us don't see this beauty very often. If you come for the sunset; you're in for an awe-inspiring treat but if at all possible, come for the sunrise and capture the view from under the pier… you'll appreciate the new perspective.

There's also a beach bar, a gift shop, and a bait shop so if you forgot it, you can buy it right there at the pier. You'll find it at 41 Fort Pickens Road and the $1.25 entry fee is oh so worth it.

5. I WANT TO GO FISHING BUT I DON'T HAVE A BOAT

Not to worry, Hot Spots Charters is the largest fishing charter operation on the Gulf Coast and they deserve every star of their five-star rating. You'll find them in Pensacola Beach, 701 Pensacola Beach Blvd., and they know EVERYTHING about fish and fishing. Whether you're an experienced angler or a family of landlubbers, the captains at Hot Spots will make your trip comfortable, memorable, and fish-full.

The moment you step on the boat, you'll be impressed with the professionalism and attentiveness of your captain (they're ALL fantastic) and once on the water, you'll be guided to hot spots of red snapper, grouper, Spanish mackerel, or whatever they know is biting that day. Kids are welcome and the captains go out of their way to include them and make their experience fish-friendly. The captains are experts at knowing what's biting, planning the day, and catering to the experience level of the fishermen aboard.

Upon return to the dock, your fish are cleaned, filleted, bagged, and put on ice for you – the ultimate ending to the perfect fishing excursion.

>TOURIST

6. JOE PATTI'S: MORE THAN JUST A FISH MARKET

Best. Shrimp. Ever. Whether it's a quick stop after your day at the beach or shopping for a well-planned meal, this place is an absolute must. Located at 524 S B. Street, Pensacola, bring the entire family… shopping for seafood here is an event.

Upon entering, you'll want to get a ticket for your place in line from the uniformed ticket-giver (sometimes accompanied by a mermaid) but don't. It doesn't matter if there are 10 or 50 customers milling around, the dozens of servers crank through orders like a machine. So, first peruse the fish counter and then get your ticket. Your number will be called in a few minutes or less.

What to get? SHRIMP... without question. I recommend both the peeled, deveined shrimp and the Royal Reds; it will be tough to choose a favorite but either way, you won't be disappointed. Be sure to pick up cocktail sauce and a tub of the garlic scampi butter from the refrigerator section to go with your shrimp; there are some unique items in the market section as well.

As you check out, the checker will ask if you want your shrimp steamed; the answer is yes. You can choose how much spice you want added to the steaming process; the shrimp is then bagged and put on ice for your trip home. (Styrofoam coolers are available for purchase if your trip home is a long one.) You'll be hooked on Joe Patti's after just one visit…guaranteed.

7. SNORKELING

Pensacola offers natural and artificial reefs and sunken ships, that can be accessed from the beaches for snorkelers. Most of the sunken vessels are in deeper waters but there are many visible when snorkeling. Nonetheless, all the reefs will entertain you with the gulf wildlife. Some nearby snorkeling options include:

• The Fort Pickens Jetty (inside Fort Pickens) is on the north side of the island and is home to a sunken tugboat and the wreck of the Norwegian Catherine. The marine life varies according to the tides and time of year.

• The old Pensacola Beach Fishing Pier is sunken to east of the new Pensacola Beach Fishing Pier and is home to sea turtles, nurse sharks and flounder. It is also a popular night diving spot.

>TOURIST

- Jacobi Reef is found west of the Pensacola Reef Fishing Pier and consists of rows of pilings populated with grouper and snapper.

Keep in mind that water temperatures vary about 20 degrees from summer to winter. Visibility and marine populations vary along with temperatures and recent storm activity.

8. ENTERING THE PENSACOLA NAVAL AIR STATION

Visiting the Pensacola NAS (or any military base) is an honor and a privilege; just know that you cannot simply drive up and expect to enter. Visitors must have a purpose and in Pensacola, when civilians may only visit the NAS Museum, the Pensacola Lighthouse, and Fort Barrancas. You will need to plan ahead:

- Entry is only through the West Gate on Blue Angel Parkway
- The gate closes to visitors at 4:30pm
- Identification is required for anyone 18 or older. Check online as SOME U.S. DRIVER'S LICENSES ARE NOT ACCEPTED and an alternate ID is required.

- Have vehicle registration and proof of insurance
- No pets allowed
- During high traffic times, lines may form and passing through the entry may be slow. If you have tour reservations, plan accordingly.
- Once you're in and headed to one of the three destinations, show extreme respect for all rules and regulations. A 15-mph speed limit does not mean 16-mph and alcohol consumption can buy you a world of trouble.

9. A LIGHTHOUSE WITH MORE THAN JUST A VIEW

Located on the Naval base at 2081 Radford Blvd., the Pensacola Lighthouse offers the most spectacular views of the area. From the top you'll see the bay, the city skyline, and the historic Navy Yard. Quite possibly, it's the best spot to experience Pensacola…don't miss this one. Also, be sure to visit the gift shop and take the nature walk to the beach. The view of the Lighthouse and surrounding area is one of the most beautiful in all of Northwest Florida.

Admission to the Lighthouse is reasonable and tours are available. Be sure to review visitation details

>TOURIST

online as height, shoe, and backpack restrictions apply to all visitors.

Visiting the Lighthouse and the Naval Museum on the same day makes a great trip. There's a delightful restaurant inside the museum, the Cubi Bar Café, which offers soups, salads, and sandwiches from 11:00 to 3:00 pm. Not just a restaurant, it's also a museum-type exhibit. Or, if you would rather dine outdoors, bring your own picnic and head over to the beach. It's just a short walk and the as always, the views are worth taking in.

10. SEE A BLUE ANGEL PRACTICE FROM THE TOP OF THE LIGHTHOUSE

If at all possible, plan to visit the Lighthouse during one of the Blue Angel practices. As you stand on the catwalk of the lighthouse, 191 feet above the ground, you can feel the incredible power of an F/A-18 Hornet and even see the pilot in the cockpit as it buzzes past. It's a heart-pounding experience not to be missed and unless you're a Blue Angel Pilot, you will NEVER get this close to a jet roaring by at nearly 700 mph.

The Blue Angels practice on Tuesdays and Wednesdays, March thru November, and reservations in the Lighthouse are limited to 15 visitors per practice. Admission during the Blue Angel practice times are $20 and reservations are required but this is a five-star event that is totally worth it. Full information and reservations are on the Pensacola Lighthouse website.

11. PEG LEG PETE'S IS WORTH THE WAIT

If you came to Pensacola, you came for seafood, and Peg Leg Pete's has it all: blackened, fried, steamed, grilled, baked, or broiled versions of nearly any fish in the Gulf and don't forget the oysters! Normally a large menu equals average food but Pete's delivers on freshness and flavor.

Located in Pensacola Beach, there is live local music every night of the summer and several nights each week during the winter. The views are delightful year-round and the atmosphere is always upbeat. Portions are large, prices are fair, and locals are frequent so you can be sure Peg Leg Pete's is a top-notch destination! You'll find Peg Leg Pete's at 1010 Ft. Pickens Rd. in Pensacola Beach.

12. IF YOU LOVE BASEBALL

The Blue Wahoos are Pensacola's minor league baseball team. Their major league team affiliation changed in 2018; they are currently the Double-A affiliate of the Minnesota Twins.

The Wahoos play at Admiral Fetterman Field in Blue Wahoo Stadium, 351 W. Cedar Street in Pensacola. The stadium is extremely family-friendly and has a unique ambiance; the harbor view gives baseball a coastal flair not found anywhere else and left-field out-of-the-park home runs end up in the water!

As AA stadiums go, this one is small with room for only about 5000 fans so seating is close to the players and the fun is even closer. There are lots of interactive between-inning events to keep things lively and the staff is extremely friendly. Also, there's a playground behind the stadium so if your little ones get restless, you can leave the park near center field and re-enter when you're ready.

The season runs April through September but in the hot summer months, bring your sunglasses, fanning devices, and light clothes… sometimes the cool bay breeze refuses to blow.

13. BEST OF THE BEST BUSHWHACKER

What's a Bushwhacker? It's a taste of Pensacola in an ice cream cocktail laden with decadent flavors of chocolate, coffee liqueur, coconut, and rum. There are good Bushwhackers and great ones; head downtown to the Tin Cow for the best one in Pensacola. There are other ice cream cocktails on the menu (there's also the non-alcoholic variety); but the Palafox Bushwhacker is the one to try and, if you're a swashbuckler, ask for a double shot; it's a party in a glass.

To go with your Bushwhacker, you have got to design your own gourmet burger. Choose your bun, your cheese, and your toppings and let your creativity run; the burgers are five-star delicious! The Tin Cow is found at 102 S. Palafox Street, downtown Pensacola.

>TOURIST

14. FORT PICKENS IS A MUST

Everyone should know a bit of Pensacola history and Fort Pickens has a story. It's a massive fort built by the U.S. Army during the Civil War and later on, it was used as a prison and even held Apache war chief, Geronimo.

Inside, you can stroll through mine chambers and prisoner quarters, climb on cannons, and explore tunnels connecting various parts of the fort. Your kids' imaginations will run wild with possibilities and you can imagine the young soldiers and the lives they led here as they fought for their beliefs.

Fort Pickens also has a campground for overnight stays. Reservations are required; there are sites with electric and water hookups as well as tent sites. Drinking water, toilets, showers, and a dump station are available. The sand dunes, the hiking trails, and the beach make camping at Fort Pickens some of the best to be found. Admission to the campground is $26 - $50/night and you'll need a reservation.

15. HOT, SANDY MUSIC

Bands on the Beach is an outdoor summer concert series featuring regional artists from a variety of genres. Located in the Gulfside Pavilion (20 Casino Beach Boardwalk, Pensacola Beach) overlooking the Gulf of Mexico, start time is 7:00 pm every Tuesday during the warm months (April through October). The music varies from high-adrenaline to smooth and laid-back; choose your band and head to the beach.

Coolers are ok to bring (just no glass); you can even bring your own tables and arrange a full-on tailgate-type experience! Or if you prefer, there are concessions nearby with food and drink options, including cocktails. Either way, bring your chairs, watch the sunset, and bob your head to the summer sounds of some hot music! Lineups of bands can be found online.

16. INCREDIBLE SCUBA DIVING

Pensacola is home to over a thousand dive spots ranging from recreational to very technical; this area is considered a premier location for scuba diving. Shipwrecks, oil rigs, airplanes, and both natural and

>TOURIST

artificial reefs are home to plentiful marine life and pieces of history.

Know your scuba self; your interests, training, and experience level will narrow your diving options to the best dive spots to match your expectations. With dozens of local dive shops, you'll want to plan well in advance to select the spot and availability of the dive you want. Do your research… knowing the story of the sunken ship you choose will further enhance your dive experience!

Pensacola's ultimate technical dive spot is The USS Oriskany, known as "the great carrier reef." As the world's largest artificial reef, it attracts top-rated divers from all over the world. The 911-foot U.S. Navy aircraft carrier sits upright on the floor of the Gulf, 22 miles off the coast. Don't expect to see this as a beginning or intermediate diver; this one requires advanced levels of training and extensive experience.

Whatever your experience level, the life and times below the surface will only serve to deepen your love for the everything Pensacola.

17. DOWNTOWN NIGHT LIFE

Put this in your phone map: 130 E. Government Street, Pensacola. The Seville Quarter is THE place for everything entertainment. The Seville is a rambling complex of seven intertwining venues with moods ranging from relaxing to raucous.

Once inside, you'll want to wander from room to room to see them all – you will find something! Then settle in for a drink, a bite, and an evening of fun.

• Rosie O'Grady's Dueling Piano Show is a musical feast
• Phineas Phogg's Balloon Works is a two-story dance club
• End O'the Alley Bar and Courtyard has live music nightly targeting young professionals
• Fast Eddie's Billiard Parlor is just as its name
• Lili Marlene's is a World War I | Aviator's Pub with karaoke on weeknights and live music on weekends
• Apple Annie's Courtyard is a lunch venue on weekdays and a dance hall Thursday-Saturday nights
• Palace Oyster Bar offers drinks and dinner Monday-Saturday

Depending on where the needle on your fun-meter sits, you'll find your spot in The Seville Quarter and

>TOURIST

breakfast, lunch, dinner, can be found at one or more of the seven spots.

18. YOU'VE GOT TO TRY A DUELING PIANO BAR

Inside the Seville Quarter, Rosie O'Grady's Dueling Piano Show is five-star FUN, FUN, FUN! Rosie's is a dueling piano bar with lively music played by the most talented piano-playing, song-singing, all-around fun people you'll find! The audience interaction is great entertainment and the fun-charged atmosphere appeals to every age.

The casual pub setting will bring out your inner singing talent as you join along with the rest of the crowd. Shows start at 8:00pm Wednesday-Saturday; drop on in… you're not too cool to sing along at Rosie O'Grady's!

19. BE THE SCENE

Sometimes you have to brave the crowds to feel the vibe. Music, food, shopping, performances, and people watching are the best elements of festival-going and Pensacola has some great fall options:

- The Pensacola Seafood Festival, the last weekend of September, offers a flavor for every palate. Sample dishes from top restaurants, watch cooking demonstrations, and shop with local vendors. Come hungry; this is a big event that spans Seville Square, Fountain Park, and Bartram Park and draws a lot of hungry sea-fooders!

- The Great Gulfcoast Arts Festival is one of the best art events in the U.S., held in early November in Seville Square. More than 200 of the best artists from around the country and the globe present their creations over a course of three days. You'll find more than just trinkets; these artists display magnificent pieces. This Festival has been named one of the Top 100 Events in North America.

- The Pensacola Beach Songwriter's Festival in early October is part of the larger Frank Brown International Songwriter's Festival. This Festival is a collection of up-close and live concert experiences found at assorted Pensacola bars and restaurants. As stories are told and songs are sung, you're an intimate part of this uniquely Pensacola music experience. The locations vary from year to year; visit the Pensacola

Beach Songwriters Festival website for all of the details.

• The Pensacola Foo Foo Fest is a collection of art and cultural events spanning 12 days. The broad scope of this Festival actually includes larger events including the Blue Angels Airshow and the Great Gulfcoast Arts Festival and there are dozens of small happenings and sights worth visiting. The smaller events vary from year to year; you'll find Science on the Street, concert and performing art presentations, and an array of eclectic entertainment options. Definitely check their website and search the dozens of options. You will find several unique options to start your November.

20. FRISKY DOLPHIN FOR THE BEST OYSTERS

When a place is a favorite of the locals, you know it's worth a visit. The Frisky Dolphin has great food, a terrific bar selection, and the prices are reasonable. Add a stunning sunset and you're set for a fantastic dinner experience! It's a come-as-you-are type place with a very casual atmosphere.

Once you head over to 715 Pensacola Beach Blvd, get to work on the oysters. You can't go wrong with the traditional raw or Rockefeller versions, but you'll want to add either the Parmesan Crusted or the Oysters Frisky (better yet, get both) to your order. After that, anything Redfish served here will impress you. It's hard to choose between the Blackened Redfish Tacos, the Redfish Sandwich, or the Redfish Frisky but any of the selections are sure to satisfy your fish fantasies, and, the Tater Tots served with the meals add a touch of fun!

If you're looking for a weekend breakfast, the Frisky Dolphin serves mimosas and bloody Marys at great prices starting at 8:00 am. Along with their delicious breakfast offerings, the views and smells of the calm morning waters are a great way to start your day.

21. THE DE LUNA WINERY

Not your typical winery, De Luna's combines fruit wine-tasting with family fun. The fruit-flavored wine blends are uniquely Pensacola; sweet wine lovers will want to sit and enjoy the flavors.

>TOURIST

The De Luna winemakers have created, evolved, and perfected their wine selections. Flavors include cherry, strawberry-kiwi, blueberry, and pomegranate and are unlike any other! As you sample, take in the Court of De Luna - a family-friendly event space where patrons can play corn hole, giant chess, giant Jenga, and more.

22. PROPER FOOTWEAR

Two words: flip flops. Pensacola's average daily daytime temperatures range from 92°F in the summer to 65°F in the winter but the footwear is constant. Flip flops are worn here by both men and women with all apparel from swimsuits to heavy jackets. Flip flops are appropriate for dining out, church, and formal events.

23. BEACH TOYS - BYO OR YOU CAN RENT

If your travel to Pensacola is in a car, plan on being crammed full with more than just your swimsuit and sunscreen; you will need chairs, coolers, toys, beach umbrellas, and towels. You will also want to add your cornhole game, the volleyball set, your bicycles and a spike ball game, but if that's just not possible, they're all available to rent. There are many rental options to choose from and depending on where you're staying, some will even deliver. Premier Adventure Park at 460 Pensacola Beach Blvd has pretty much everything.

24. HEAD EAST ON SANTA ROSA ISLAND

"I had no idea this was here!" is what every first-time visitor says. Santa Rosa Island is the barrier island that includes Pensacola Beach and extends 40 miles east through the town of Navarre and on toward Destin.

Pensacola Beach is a beautiful part of the island but as you head east out of town, it becomes even more idyllic. Heading east on 399 out of town (it's the only road), you will pass hotels, condos, and beach houses. As they thin out, start slowing down; you'll want to catch every glimpse of the Gulf and its exquisite beauty. As you drive, the sand is whiter, the water is bluer, and your mood is better than ever. It's just that incredible.

>TOURIST

Bring your camera, bring your phone; you'll never have enough shots of the turquoise blue water and the sugar white sand. You'll find fewer fellow tourists and possibly even a rare moment with the entire beach to yourself. As you continue, there are designated parking areas on the south side; you'll want to stop at ALL of them to drink in the absolute glory of this Gulf Coast shoreline and let the world stand still for a moment.

"Leave Only Your Footprints" is the local beach motto. As you absorb the magnificence of Santa Rosa Island beaches, you'll have no trouble complying with this saying. Most of the area is Gulf Islands National Seashore and is protected from commercial development so you'll be satisfied in knowing the pristine beauty will remain unchanged for future generations. Footprints are welcome.

25. NAVARRE BEACH

Nuh - VAHR. A divine, white-sanded, emerald-watered area of the Gulf, eighteen miles east of Pensacola Beach. Located about half way between Pensacola Beach and Destin, it is far less crowded than the better-known beach towns and Navarre

Beach is another beach that will leave you thinking, "Am I in the Caribbean?"

Navarre also has a fishing/sightseeing pier, even longer than the Pensacola Beach option. For $1.00, it's the best place to view both the sunrise and the sunset. The fishing is excellent ($7.00 fee) and sightings of sea turtles, sting rays, sharks, and dolphin are common.

Unlike some area beaches, most of Navarre Beach is not set in front of condos or beach houses. Backed by white sanded dunes with swaying sea grass, your views from this piece paradise span 360°.

26. PENSACOLA NAS MUSEUM

Don't pass this up because "I don't do museums." The National Naval Aviation Museum will leave you in awe of our country's military and aerospace aircraft and the aviators who fly them. Standing beneath an actual fighter jet that engaged in combat is moving; reading the stories of men and women who flew them or sacrificed their lives is humbling. This museum is an emotional experience not to be missed.

The Museum displays over 150 authentic aircraft, including a previous version of "Fat Albert," the

>TOURIST

enormous C-130 Hercules logistics plane (this guy can haul over 20 tons of equipment!).

If you browse all 4000 exhibits, you'll want to stop at the Cubi Point Café. It's inside the museum, is open for lunch, and displays additional memorabilia. If you're looking for souvenirs, the Flight Deck Store is where you can find your Blue Angel t-shirt.

Be sure to use the West Entrance to the Navy base on Blue Angel Parkway, the guards will turn you away from all other gates.

27. IF YOU'VE NEVER SEEN AN AIRSHOW

The Blue Angels, the Navy's flight demonstration team are the pride of Pensacola and should be experienced at least once in a lifetime. The Blue Angels practices may be seen practicing maneuvers over the NAS Museum, usually on Tuesdays and Wednesdays throughout the year; check the schedule in advance to plan your visit.

GET TO AN AIRSHOW. Pensacola Beach hosts the Blue Angels every year in July – this is not to be missed! When locals visit an event every single year, you know it's worthwhile and watching this show is unforgettable. The beauty of the Gulf of Mexico coupled with maneuvers of the F/A-18 Hornets is flat out jaw-dropping.

Getting to the show requires advance planning as parking is the problem for you and tens of thousands of others. However, there are four possible solutions:

1. Arrive in advance (six hours prior is not unreasonable). You'll be on the beach anyway so the day is a double bonus.

2. Take a ferry to the beach (check the Pensacola Bay Ferry System).

3. Park far away. The jets fly up and down the beach for miles so you will see them and you're still on the beach.

4. Attend the practice show the day before. It's the exact same show with slightly less attendance. The viewing locations are exactly the same as on Airshow day.

The November Blue Angel Homecoming Air Show at the NAS is equally impressive and includes an extensive ground display of dozens of aircraft. You'll be able to view all of the air acrobatics with general admission but for an even better experience, tickets can be purchased in advance for prime seating areas. Same rules for entering the navy base apply; same thrilling experience will occur. Even if you

>TOURIST

attended the Pensacola Beach Air Show, this is worth taking in also.

28. THESE PELICANS WON'T FLY AWAY

"Pelicans in Paradise" is a public art display featuring dozens of five-foot fiberglass pelicans dotted throughout historic downtown (inspired by the collection of cow statues in downtown Portland, OR). Created by local artists, the brightly colored statues have various themes and the downtown square showcases birds honoring the four branches of the military. Depending on how many statues are "in the shop" for maintenance, you will find roughly 60 statues.

If your hope is to stroll Pensacola to see every statue, you will wear yourself out. They are located at various locations around town and some are miles apart. Searching for all of the pelicans should be done on wheels. There is a listing of the pelicans' locations online, along with their geo-coordinates.

29. SHOPPING ON PALAFOX

Big city dwellers may think our downtown is small and our main street is short but hold on… we have southern charm. Pensacola's Palafox Street has been on more than one list of "Great Streets in America" and for good reason.

The architecture, sidewalks, foliage, and the plazas display the artistic beauty of the south, but without big city traffic. Your pace will slow as you take in the views (or it may be due to the leisurely speed of the people in front of you). The shopping options are varied and include contemporary jewelry, eclectic furnishings, fine art, casual dining, trendy clothing, or just plain beer. Everybody loves something so slow down, glance in the windows, and watch for it…you'll find it on Palafox Street.

Stop in Urban Objects - at least to see the light fixtures, visit Innerlight Surf Shop for trendy surf and skate products, and end up at World of Beer for a cold brew. There are dozens of shops and restaurants centrally located; stop and shop a few!

Continue south on Palafox and you'll come upon the Ruby Slipper. Three words: Gourmet. Southern. Breakfast. Not just your eggs and bacon kind of place, the Ruby Slipper offers New Orleans-inspired gourmet delights. Start with some of Ruby's fabulous coffee (or maybe a bloody Mary). Choosing between the eggs benedict plates or the omelets will be difficult but either way, you can't go wrong.

Palafox Street will make you love Pensacola even more.

30. JACO'S FOR DINING DELUXE

Jaco's Bayfront Bar & Grill, 997 S. Palafox Street, Pensacola, is a casual indulgence where you can linger for hours. The waterfront location on the Inner Harbor Channel has both indoor and outdoor tables, and weather permitting, you'll want to sit outside for a view of the sparkling water (and some pretty impressive yachts at the adjacent marina).

Once you're seated, open the menu and head straightaway to the featured cocktails. The drinks are upscaled variations of boozy favorites; if rum is your passion, try the Old Cuban.

You can't go wrong with any selection on the menu; the flavors are adventuresome and the creativity is first-rate. What to order? Don't be fooled by the informal name, Jaco's Tacos are a gourmet presentation of savory Mahi complemented with Mango Salsa.

If you've come this far, add dessert (go for the Fried Oreos) and stay for a while longer. Chances are, you're intoxicated by the view and your mind is wondering, "What would I name my yacht?"

31. WATERSPORTS RENTALS

Sometimes you have to go beyond sitting on the beach or splashing near the sand; you need to get out beyond the first 100 yards and there are so many ways to do it!

DON'T BE AFRAID TO RENT A PONTOON BOAT. The only license required is your driver's license and these big boys are a world of fun! You will be shown everything you need to know to operate the pontoon and rentals are available for full or half days. Cruise, swim, picnic, and have a blast with your group; there are even tiki hut-type boats with a slide from the upper deck directly to the water. Grab your friends and rent a pontoon… it's oh so worth it! Be sure to reserve online in advance, pontoon rentals are popular so don't miss out.

>TOURIST

Stand up paddleboards (SUPs), kayaks, jet skis, parasailing, and sailboats will all get you out on the water. Choose your water speed preference and apply your sunscreen because the options to get out on the water are endless in Pensacola Beach. The rental facilities are easy to find; try Pensacola Beach Pontoon Boat Rentals, Radical Rides, or Key Sailing to rent equipment or book a tour.

32. A DOLPHIN CRUISE IS WORTH THE MONEY

A local cruise is a fantastic way to explore the waters of Pensacola Bay, Santa Rosa Sound, and the Gulf of Mexico. Tours vary by destination, boat size and speed (and amenities aboard), time of day, what you want to see, and of course how much you want to spend.

and For the most part, dolphin sightings are the highlight of the cruise captains know where to find the best spots for viewing. Of course there are rare times when the dolphins don't fully cooperate but any sighting is a good one… everyone loves a dolphin!

The cruise experience is generally a family-friendly party atmosphere, with drinks, snacks, and an entertaining crew who go out of their way to provide an exceptional experience for all. Come as a single and leave with new friends!

Besides a dolphin-specific outing, other options include sunset cruises, trips with beach stops, and Blue Angel viewing cruises. There is also a scenic sightseeing tour of Pensacola where you will cruise along the National Seashore and pass by landmarks like Fort Pickens, NAS Pensacola, the Naval Aviation Museum, and the Pensacola Lighthouse. Reservations are definitely required and all information needed is available online.

33. GHOST HUNTING IN PENSACOLA

Pensacola is home to a great deal of haunted history and modern-day paranormal activity. The Pensacola Lighthouse on the NAS is said to be one of the most haunted lighthouses in the United States and has even been featured on the Travel Channel.

If you would like to feel the supernatural or do a bit of ghost hunting on your own, the Lighthouse can accommodate you. The Pensacola Lighthouse Paranormal Team present the Lighthouse Ghost Hunt

>TOURIST

during which you can experience the extraordinary and draw your own conclusions.

The tour is a bit of dark fun and explores the haunted past of the Lighthouse and the area. This adventure is offered twice monthly (sometimes more often) during the summer months, April thru November. The tour begins at 8:30 pm and is limited to ages 12 and over. Reservations are absolutely required as the tour is on the Naval Base and anyone entering after business hours must have an escort. Reservations can be made on the Lighthouse website or by calling the Lighthouse directly.

34. PENSACOLA HISTORICAL TIDBITS

Impress your friends, family, or maybe your restaurant server with useful and relevant Pensacola facts:

• It is said that Pensacola was named after a region called Panzacola, meaning "long-haired people".

• The white beach sand is actually white quartz sand washed down from the Appalachian Mountains via the Apalachicola River.

- Over the course of history, the city has had been represented by five groups: Spain, France, Britain, the Confederacy, and the United States of America. These are known as the Five Flags of Pensacola.
- American pioneer, Daniel Boone wanted to settle in Pensacola but his wife refused to leave North Carolina.
- St. Augustine (northeast coast) may not be the oldest city in America. Researchers say they have evidence that Spanish Explorer, Don Tristan de Luna established his colony of Pensacola six years before its coastal cousin.
- It is unlawful to run out of fuel on the Pensacola Three Mile Bridge.
- Typically, Florida is not classified as part of the Deep South. States once dependent on plantations, also known as Cotton States are part of this distinction but since Northwest Florida has deep history with cotton plantations, it's included in the classification.
- The first Catholic Mass in the United States was held on Pensacola Beach in 1559. The location is marked by a small cross on a sandy hillside just west of the Beach Ball Tower.

>TOURIST

35. GREAT GREEK FLAVORS TO GO

Shoreline Foods International Market & Deli is a family business with truly authentic Greek flavors. Hidden in a residential area near the Harbor, it's easy to drive right past this unassuming store front.

While Shoreline does not offer the lighting, sights, and scents of a gourmet grocery store, the selection of imported Greek olives, oils, spreads, and spices is extensive and there is a large selection of Greek wines as well. There is also a deli counter offering made-to-order hot sandwiches and salads. (There is no dining area so all orders are take-out only.)

How about a decadent Greek picnic? Fill your basket with a loaf of olive bread and crackers, a jar of olive spread, and two tubs of olives (one black, one green). You'll want to add a gyro sandwich from the deli, a bottle of wine, and a pastry from the refrigerator; you're ready for your own personal Greek-fest!

36. PENSACON

Pensacon is the Southeast version of the original Comic-Con. It's a multi-genre entertainment and comic convention which attracts fans of sci-fi, fantasy, gaming, horror, anime, and beyond. The convention features celebrities, cosplay celebrities, artists, special effects experts, and more. "Wild fun" just begins to describe the three-day event.

The Pensacola Comic Con Convention has exploded over the past few years and attendance continues to grow. Presented each year in February, Pensacon encompasses a number of venues, including the Pensacola Bay Center, the Pensacola Grand Hotel, Saenger Theater, and others, depending on the occasion.

Step out of your norm; get your costume and head over to Pensacon. Better than Halloween, it's a chance to let your alter ego surface. Full details are available on the Pensacon website.

>TOURIST

37. SOUNDS INTERESTING... MAYBE I'LL DRIVE BY

• There's a car on the roof at Capt'n Fun Beach Club.
    400 Quietwater Beach Rd., Pensacola Beach
• The Futuro House resembles a UFO.
    1304 Panferio Dr., Pensacola Beach
• This Dome Home can withstand 300 mph winds.
    1005 Ariola Drive, Pensacola Beach
• The Crystal Ice House is made of stucco to resemble icicles.
    2024 Davis Street, Pensacola
• Goofy Golf is one of the country's oldest miniature golf courses and has a 12 ft. concrete t-Rex dinosaur.
    3924 W. Navy Blvd., Pensacola

38. HISTORIC PENSACOLA

Pensacola has some remarkable history and there's a lot to be learned at the Historic Pensacola Village. Situated in a shady area near Pensacola Bay, the Village includes twenty-some properties belonging to the Pensacola National Register Historic District and spans over four square blocks. This area is an interesting draw for history lovers or anyone looking for an alternative to hot sun or rainy afternoons.

The T.T. Wentworth Jr. Florida State Museum is the anchor facility of the area, 120 Church Street, Pensacola, and houses many unique exhibits including The City of Five Flags, a Trader Jon's display, and an eclectic collection from T.T. Wentworth himself.

Guided tours are available (and are required for some areas) and local associates are dressed in period costumes. Admission also gains entry into the Museum of Commerce and Museum of Industry, the Children's Museum, and others. Tickets are good for one week so if you choose to make your visit a quick one, you can always come back. Several dining options are also located nearby.

>TOURIST

39. WALL SOUTH VIETNAM MEMORIAL

Wall South is Pensacola's tribute to those who sacrificed their lives in the Vietnam War. The Memorial is a half-scale replica of the original Washington D.C. version and has the same 58,315 names of dead and missing soldiers. If you have not had the privilege of viewing the Washington D.C. version, Wall South is every bit as moving.

Wall South is located in the Veterans Memorial Park at E. Romana street & Bayfront Parkway, Pensacola. The Park also features shrines to the American Revolution, the Korean War, WWI, WWII, and the War on Terror. In addition to other memorials and tributes, the park houses the Marine Corp Bell Tower. Your patriotism will surface with the beauty of this park.

40. A HARDWARE STORE THAT'S NOT ALL HARDWARE

Looking for some interesting shopping? Pensacola Hardware Company is your target. Located downtown at 20 E. Gregory Street, it's one of Pensacola's oldest and longest running businesses.

Aside from a broad inventory of typical hardware and construction supplies, the selection of quality cookware, dining accessories, and housewares is definitely browse-worthy. You're sure to find something you need (or just want) amongst the huge selection of upscale gifts and gadgets.

41. YOU'LL GO NUTS AT THE RENFROE PECAN COMPANY

Pecans are a staple of the south and the people at the J.W. Renfroe Pecan Company, 2400 West Fairfield Drive in Pensacola, have the best. Renfroe's has been in Pensacola for over 50 years and their store is a must to put on your list of places to visit.

More than just basic nuts, there are dozens of flavor-coated pecans (you've got to try the Chocolate Amaretto), preserves, coffees, cookies, and fudge (you can't leave without fudge). The store also carries a classy selection of coastal themed, Pensacola-related non-edible gifts. You will want to bring a piece of Renfroe's (and Pensacola) home with you.

>TOURIST

42. PIZZA PIZZA

There can never be just one great pizza place in any city; Pensacola is another spot with many great options:

• Head downtown to 3000 E. Cervantes St. for some of Pensacola's best. Georgio's was founded by a Greek restauranteur and the old-world pride of cooking remains today. Artisan crusts are stacked high with fresh toppings and crowned with mounds of cheese; I like the Don Diego - gyro meat, feta, and onions on a thin crust.

• Tuscan Oven Pizzeria, 4801 9th Ave., has traditional favorites cooked in their wood-fired oven. The thick dough is tasty and the toppings are generous. You can't miss with the traditional Margherita Pizza.

• Try out the Ozone Pizza Pub, 1010 N. 12th Ave., Pensacola. The repurposed hospital location is both cozy and weird; the pizza is delicious. The Crazy Horse Pizza with chipotle marinara, chorizo, and cheddar & monterey jack cheeses is as unique as the place!

43. YOU'RE CLOSE TO L.A.

You may hear locals claim to work in Pensacola and live in L.A. It's not quite the commute you might think; Lower Alabama is fifteen miles from downtown. The Southern drawl heard in these parts will not be heard in the other L.A.

44. #1 BEACH BAR IN THE U.S.A.

If you're going toward L.A., plan on stopping at the Flora-Bama. Straddling the state line between Florida and Alabama, this world-famous spot is one of a kind. The Flora-Bama is a beach bar, a honky-tonk, a roadhouse, and an oyster bar… but mostly, it's a MUST. Is it a tourist destination? Yes. Do tourists love it? Absolutely.

First, it's family friendly; kids are welcome until 6:00pm. Bring the family through the doors to the beach side (just no coolers) and make it a day! After 6:00pm, the minimum age is 18 and a cover charge is added.

Next, don't expect posh – the Flora-Bama has character. The walls are crammed with memorabilia, signs, graffiti, and pretty much anything you can

>TOURIST

think of, none of which can be described as upscale. It's a curious feast for the eyes.

Finally, there is something for everyone. To name a few, the sprawling complex has bingo, dancing, pool tables, bars, TVs, and music – a lot of music. There are live performances on five different stages 365 days a year; you're sure to find one or more that you like. As for drinks, if you're not sure where to begin, start with the Flora-Bama Bushwhacker or the Key Lime Daquiri. Both options are sure to get your mind open and your foot tapping.

The Flora-Bama is world-famous for events. In addition to the daily activities, there are the legendary annual events. The Mullet Toss, the Fishing Rodeo, the Bikini Contest, and the All-American Barbeque are spring/summer favorites while Bulls on the Beach and the Polar Bear Dip are winter draws. The fun is large and the crowds are dense so arrive early and claim your spot.

Finally, the concert lineup brings in huge names each year. Check the schedule; you'll want and need tickets in advance. All of these dates draw huge crowds so be prepared; parking and visibility may be challenging. The Flora-Bama address is 17401 Perdido Key Dr., Pensacola, FL.

45. KNOW YOUR BEACH FLAGS AND RIP CURRENTS

Pensacola's public beaches display flags up and down the sand to alert you of water conditions. Especially if you're bringing little ones to the beach, it's best to know what to expect before you enter the water.

- Green – generally calm water; ok to swim
- Yellow – moderate surf and/or currents may be present; be careful
- Red – severe hazard and dangerous rough currents; no swimming or wading. Entering water displaying a red flag is illegal in Escambia County
- Double Red – extreme danger, water is closed. Used only during hurricanes or other natural disasters. Entering water displaying a double red flag is illegal in Escambia County.
- Blue or Purple – jellyfish, sharks, or other dangerous marine life has been spotted. Use extra caution anywhere in or near the water.

Also, everyone should be aware of rip currents. These are formed when water rushes back out to sea in a narrow path. Rip currents are turbulent, fast-

>TOURIST

flowing, and dangerous; they can carry a swimmer away from shore very quickly. They may appear as:
- a different water color – darker or murkier
- larger or choppier waves
- a bowl-shaped indentation in the surf
- foam or vegetation, usually perpendicular to the shore

Beware of rip currents. They are a real phenomenon on Pensacola beaches so always use caution and avoid any of these conditions.

46. AN IRISH, IRISH PUB

McGuire's Irish Pub offers everything you want in an Irish fun spot – great Irish pub-style food, lively music, and a party-crowd atmosphere. This restaurant is located at 600 E. Gregory Street in Pensacola and is five-star rated. It may be crowded with a line out the door but it's worth the wait (they don't take reservations but use the "Nowait" app).

Whether you go for lunch, brunch, or dinner, you will find something you love. The menu is not overcrowded with selections so everything served is done well. The Senate Bean Soup is wildly popular but if you love Reubens, try the Reuben Eggroll.

Known for their steaks (one of the few places in America to serve U.S.D.A. Certified Prime cuts), McGuire's delivers in excellence on any of their grilled cuts. Or, if you're looking for true Irish fare, the Shepherd's Pie is delicious… and huge!

Given the large portions, dessert can be difficult to fit. Nonetheless, you've got to fit in an Irish Coffee. The frozen version will complete your McGuire's experience and you'll leave with an Irish smile on your face.

47. A FLOUNDER DINING ADVENTURE

Bring your appetite and stay a while; Flounder's Chowder House is a celebration of Pensacola! Named for the founding family, the food is legendary and the scenery is a visual park. There is indoor and outdoor seating, an enormous beach playground, and plenty of historic memorabilia. More than just atmosphere, the menu has extraordinary offerings.

Starting out, I recommend the Diesel Fuel (try the mango) but just know that you'll need a food option to counteract the effects! It's so hard to choose one option on the Flounder's menu but the Baked Oysters

>TOURIST

appetizer and the Classic Stuffed Flounder earn my excellent review and the Key Lime Pie is the biggest serving ever. The portions are enormous so your lunch for tomorrow may be more of what you have tonight.

Adjacent to the restaurant, the Flounder's gift shop is worth a stop. The selection of shirts, supplies, and souvenirs is enormous and the collection of eclectic coastal furnishings is tasteful and classy. There is even a liquor section in the back of the store. Even if you're not dining at the restaurant, this gift shop is worth a stop.

You'll find Flounder's in Pensacola Beach just over the bridge 800 Quietwater Beach Road,

48. RIVER OPTIONS

Need some cooler waters? Tubing, canoeing, paddle boarding, and kayaking can be found in Coldwater Creek, just an hour northeast of Pensacola.

The team at Adventures Unlimited offers short trips, long trips, overnight river trips and pretty much any trip you can think of; just choose your vessel and make a plan (they also have zip lining). Adventures Unlimited will outfit you with everything you'll need (except for your snacks and drinks) but be sure to plan in advance and scour rental details on their website. There is a lot of information to be aware of before you go.

Enter 8974 Tomahawk Landing Rd., Milton, FL into your phone map to get to the start of your river excursion. Once you're on your river adventure, you will love the expedition through pristine forest areas where you can stop, sun, and picnic at even more white sand beaches along the way.

49. THE OLD HICKORY WHISKEY BAR

This place is small in size but big on character and the selections of whiskey are second to none. With over 650 whiskey offerings, the options are endless. The mixologists are extremely knowledgeable and can share the history and character of any of your options. (Be sure to ask them to relate the differences between whiskey, bourbon, and scotch.)

The Old Hickory is one place where you should definitely engage the bartender in your business. By discussing your tastes and preferences (even if it's not whiskey), you can be guided to new drink experience that just may end up to be your new personal favorite! You can find the Old Hickory at 123 Palafox Place, downtown Pensacola.

50. BOCCE BALL MAKES FRIENDS

For as beautiful as the beach is, it's even better when shared with friends. Over the years, I've made friends on the beach with people of all ages; some friendships lasted an afternoon, others have continued for years. Several of these friendships were started as I played Bocce Ball on the beach. As people watch, they are intrigued with the ball-hurling activity and aren't afraid to approach and ask, "what is that game?"

It's a simple game with eight large balls (two colors) and one small target ball. Teams toss the target ball and then lob the heavier balls toward the target, with points awarded for those being closest. This laid-back beach game can go on for hours as it moves up and down the beach, with or without cocktails in hand. It always turns heads as people are curious to know how the game works.

Get yourself a Bocce Ball game (sets can be found at nearly every store you can think of), head to the beach, and make some friends. We're here in Pensacola waiting for you.

>TOURIST

TOP REASONS TO BOOK THIS TRIP

1. We have white sugar sand and turquoise blue water.
2. It's not too crowded on our white sugar sand and turquoise blue water.
3. Two tanks of gas can get you here from most anywhere in the southeast or mid-U.S.A.
4. We have abundant great seafood.
5. We have the Blue Angels
6. The marine life is easy to find for viewing or fishing.
7. We have very water activity you can dream of.
8. It's easy to make friends in the South.

OTHER RESOURCES:

VisitPensacola.com

\>TOURIST

BONUS BOOK

50 THINGS TO KNOW ABOUT PACKING LIGHT FOR TRAVEL

PACK THE RIGHT WAY EVERY TIME

AUTHOR: MANIDIPA BHATTACHARYYA

First Published in 2015 by Dr. Lisa Rusczyk. Copyright 2015. All Rights Reserved. No part of this publication may be reproduced, including scanning and photocopying, or distributed in any form or by any means, electronic or mechanical, or stored in a database or retrieval system without prior written permission from the publisher.

Disclaimer: The publisher has put forth an effort in preparing and arranging this book. The information provided herein by the author is provided "as is". Use this information at your own risk. The publisher is not a licensed doctor. Consult your doctor before engaging in any medical activities. The publisher and author disclaim any liabilities for any loss of profit or commercial or personal damages resulting from the information contained in this book.

Edited by Melanie Howthorne

ABOUT THE AUTHOR

Manidipa Bhattacharyya is a creative writer and editor, with an education in English literature and Linguistics. After working in the IT industry for seven long years she decided to call it quits and follow her heart instead. Manidipa has been ghost writing, editing, proof reading and doing secondary research services for many story tellers and article writers for about three years. She stays in Kolkata, India with her husband and a busy two year old. In her own time Manidipa enjoys travelling, photography and writing flash fiction.

Manidipa believes in travelling light and never carries anything that she couldn't haul herself on a trip. However, travelling with her child changed the scenario. She seemed to carry the entire world with her for the baby on the first two trips. But good sense prevailed and she is again working her way to becoming a light traveler, this time with a kid.

>TOURIST

INTRODUCTION

*He who would travel happily
must travel light.*

-Antoine de Saint-Exupéry

Travel takes you to different places from seas and mountains to deserts and much more. In your travels you get to interact with different people and their cultures. You will, however, enjoy the sights and interact positively with these new people even more, if you are travelling light.

When you travel light your mind can be free from worry about your belongings. You do not have to spend precious vacation time waiting for your luggage to arrive after a long flight. There is be no chance of your bags going missing and the best part is that you need not pay a fee for checked baggage.

People who have mastered this art of packing light will root for you to take only one carry-on, wherever you go. However, many people can find it really hard to pack light. More so if you are travelling with children. Differentiating between "must have" and "just in case" items is the starting point. There will be ample shopping avenues at your destination which are just waiting to be explored.

This book will show you 'packing' in a new 'light' – pun intended – and help you to embrace light packing practices for all of your future travels.

Off to packing!

DEDICATION

I dedicate this book to all the travel buffs that I know, who have given me great insights into the contents of their backpacks.

THE RIGHT TRAVEL GEAR

1. CHOOSE YOUR TRAVEL GEAR CAREFULLY

While selecting your travel gear, pick items that are light weight, durable and most importantly, easy to carry. There are cases with wheels so you can drag them along – these are usually on the heavy side because of the trolley. Alternatively a backpack that you can carry comfortably on your back, or even a duffel bag that you can carry easily by hand or sling across your body are also great options. Whatever you choose, one thing to keep in mind is that the luggage itself should not weigh a ton, this will give you the flexibility to bring along one extra pair of shoes if you so desire.

>TOURIST

2. CARRY THE MINIMUM NUMBER OF BAGS

Selecting light weight luggage is not everything. You need to restrict the number of bags you carry as well. One carry-on size bag is ideal for light travel. Most carriers allow one cabin baggage plus one purse, handbag or camera bag as long as it slides under the seat in front. So technically, you can carry two items of luggage without checking them in.

3. PACK ONE EXTRA BAG

Always pack one extra empty bag along with your essential items. This could be a very light weight duffel bag or even a sturdy tote bag which takes up minimal space. In the event that you end up buying a lot of souvenirs, you already have a handy bag to stuff all that into and do not have to spend time hunting for an appropriate bag.

> *I'm very strict with my packing and have everything in its right place. I never change a rule. I hardly use anything in the hotel room. I wheel my own wardrobe in and that's it.*
>
> Charlie Watts

CLOTHES & ACCESSORIES

4. PLAN AHEAD

Figure out in advance what you plan to do on your trip. That will help you to pick that one dress you need for the occasion. If you are going to attend a wedding then you have to carry formal wear. If not, you can ditch the gown for something lighter that will be comfortable during long walks or on the beach.

5. WEAR THAT JACKET

Remember that wearing items will not add extra luggage for your air travel. So wear that bulky jacket that you plan to carry for your trip. This saves space and can also help keep you warm during the chilly flight.

6. MIX AND MATCH

Carry clothes that can be interchangeably used to reinvent your look. Find one top that goes well with a couple of pairs of pants or skirts. Use tops, shirts and jackets wisely along with other accessories like a scarf or a stole to create a new look.

>TOURIST

7. CHOOSE YOUR FABRIC WISELY

Stuffing clothes in cramped bags definitely takes its toll which results in wrinkles. It is best to carry wrinkle free, synthetic clothes or merino tops. This will eliminate the need for that small iron you usually bring along.

8. DITCH CLOTHES PACK UNDERWEAR

Pack more underwear and socks. These are the things that will give you a fresh feel even if you do not get a chance to wear fresh clothes. Moreover these are easy to wash and can be dried inside the hotel room itself.

9. CHOOSE DARK OVER LIGHT

While picking your clothes choose dark coloured ones. They are easy to colour coordinate and can last longer before needing a wash. Accidental food spills and dirt from the road are less visible on darker clothes.

10. WEAR YOUR JEANS

Take only one pair of Jeans with you, which you should wear on the flight. Remember to pick a pair that can be worn for sightseeing trips and is equally eloquent for dinner. You can add variety by adding light weight cargoes and chinos.

11. CARRY SMART ACCESSORIES

The right accessory can give you a fresh look even with the same old dress. An intelligent neck-piece, a couple of bright scarves, stoles or a sarong can be used in a number of ways to add variety to your clothing. These light weight beauties can double up as a nursing cover, a light blanket, beach wear, a modesty cover for visiting places of worship, and also makes for an enthralling game of peek-a-boo.

12. LEARN TO FOLD YOUR GARMENTS

Seasoned travellers all swear by rolling their clothes for compact and wrinkle free packing. Bundle packing, where you roll the clothes around a central object as if tying it up, is also a popular method of compact and wrinkle free packing. Stacking folded clothes one on top of another is a big no-no as it makes creases extreme and they are difficult to get rid of without ironing.

>TOURIST

13. WASH YOUR DIRTY LAUNDRY

One of the ways to avoid carrying loads of clothes is to wash the clothes you carry. At some places you might get to use the laundry services or a Laundromat but if you are in a pinch, best solution is to wash them yourself. If that is the plan then carrying quick drying clothes is highly recommended, which most often also happen to be the wrinkle free variety.

14. LEAVE THOSE TOWELS BEHIND

Regular towels take up a lot of space, are heavy and take ages to dry out. If you are staying at hotels they will provide you with towels anyway. If you are travelling to a remote place, where the availability of towels look doubtful, carry a light weight travel towel of viscose material to do the job.

15. USE A COMPRESSION BAG

Compression bags are getting lots of recommendation now days from regular travellers. These are useful for saving space in your luggage when you have to pack bulky dresses. While packing for the return trip, get help from the hotel staff to arrange a vacuum cleaner.

FOOTWEAR

16. PUT ON YOUR HIKING BOOTS

If you have plans to go hiking or trekking during your trip, you will need those bulky hiking boots. The best way to carry them is to wear them on flight to save space and luggage weight. You can remove the boots once inside and be comfortable in your socks.

17. PICKING THE RIGHT SHOES

Shoes are often the bulkiest items, along with being the dainty if you are a female. They need care and take up a lot of space in your luggage. It is advisable therefore to pick shoes very carefully. If you plan to do a lot of walking and site seeing, then wearing a pair of comfortable walking shoes are a must. For more formal occasions you can carry durable, light weight flats which will not take up much space.

18. STUFF SHOES

If you happen to pack a pair of shoes, ensure you utilize their hollow insides. Tuck small items like rolled up socks or belts to save space. They will also be easy to find.

>TOURIST

TOILETRIES

19. STASHING TOILETRIES

Carry only absolute necessities. Airline rules dictate that for one carry-on bag, liquids and gels must be in 3.4 ounce (100ml) bottles or less, and must be packed in a one quart zip-lock bag. If you are planning to stay in a hotel, the basic things will be provided for you. It's best is to buy the rest from the local market at your destination.

20. TAKE ALONG TAMPONS

Tampons are a hard to find item in a lot of countries. Figure out how many you need and pack accordingly. For longer stays you can buy them online and have them delivered to where you are staying.

21. GET PAMPERED BEFORE YOU TRAVEL

Some avid travellers suggest getting a pedicure and manicure just the day before travelling. This not only gives you a well kept look, you also save the trouble of packing nail polish. Remember, every little bit of weight reduced adds up.

ELECTRONICS

22. LUGGING ALONG ELECTRONICS

Electronics have a large role to play in our lives today. Most of us cannot imagine our lives away from our phones, laptops or tablets. However while travelling, one must consider the amount of weight these electronics add to our luggage. Thankfully smart phones come along with all the essentials tools like a camera, email access, picture editing tools and more. They are smart to the point of eliminating the need to carry multiple gadgets. Choose a smart phone that suits all your requirements and travel with the world in your palms or pocket.

23. REDUCE THE NUMBER OF CHARGERS

If you do travel with multiple electronic devices, you will have to bear the additional burden of carrying all their chargers too. Check if a single charger can be used for multiple devices. You might also consider investing in a pocket charger. These small devices support multiple devices while keeping you charged on the go.

24. TRAVEL FRIENDLY APPS

Along with smart phones come numerous apps, which are immensely helpful in our travels. You name it and you have an app for it at hand – take pictures, sharing with friends and family, torch to light dark roads, maps, checking flight/train times, find hotels and many other things. Use these smart alternatives to traditional items like books to eliminate weight and save space.

> *I get ideas about what's essential when packing my suitcase.*
>
> -Diane von Furstenberg

TRAVELLING WITH KIDS

25. BRING ALONG THE STROLLER

Kids might enjoy walking for a while but they soon tire out and a stroller is the just the right thing for them to rest in while you continue your tour. Strollers also double duty as a luggage carrier and shopping bag holder. Remember to pick a light weight, easy to handle brand of stroller. Better yet, find out in advance if you can rent a stroller at your destination.

26. BRING ONLY ENOUGH DIAPERS FOR YOUR TRIP

Diapers take up a lot of space and add to the weight of your luggage. Therefore it is advisable to carry just enough diapers to last through the trip and a few for afterwards, till you buy fresh stock at your destination. Unless of course you are travelling to a really remote area, in which case you have no choice but to carry the load. Otherwise diapers are something you will find pretty easily.

27. TAKE ONLY A COUPLE OF TOYS

Children are easily attracted by new things in their environment. While travelling they will find numerous 'new' objects to scrutinize and play with. Packing just one favorite toy is enough, or if there is no favorite toy leave out all of them in favor of stories or imaginary games.

28. CARRY KID FRIENDLY SNACKS

Create a small snack counter in your bag to store away quick bites for those sudden hunger pangs. Depending on the child's age this could include chocolates, raisins, dry fruits, granola bars or biscuits. Also keep a bottle of water handy for your little one.

>TOURIST

These things do not add much weight and can be adjusted in a handbag or knapsack.

29. GAMES TO CARRY

Create some travel specific, imaginary games if you have slightly grown up children, like spot the attractions. Keep a coloring book and colors handy for in-flight or hotel time. Apps on your smart phone can keep the children engaged with cartoons and story books. Older children are often entertained by games available on phones or tablets. This cuts the weight of luggage down while keeping the kids entertained.

30. LET THE KIDS CARRY THEIR LOAD

A good thing is to start early sharing of responsibilities. Let your child pick a bag of his or her choice and pack it themselves. Keep tabs on what they are stuffing in their bags by asking if they will be using that item on the trip. It could start out being just an entertainment bag initially but with growing years they will learn to sort the useful from the superfluous. Children as little as four can maneuver a small trolley suitcase like a pro- their experience in pull along toys credit. If you are worried that you may be pulling it for them, you may want to start with a backpack.

31. DECIDE ON LOCATION FOR CHILDREN TO SLEEP

While on a trip you might not always get a crib at your destination, and carrying one will make life all the more difficult. Instead call ahead to see if there are any cribs or roll out beds for children. You may even put blankets on the floor. Weave them a story about camping and they will gladly sleep without any trouble.

32. GET BABY PRODUCTS DELIVERED AT YOUR DESTINATION

If you are absolutely paranoid about not getting your favourite variety of diaper or brand of baby food, check out online stores like amazon.com for services in your destination city. You can buy things online ahead of your travel and get them delivered to your hotel upon arrival.

33. FEEDING NEEDS OF YOUR INFANTS

If you are travelling with a breastfed infant, you save the trouble of carrying bottles and bottle sanitization kits. For special food, or medications, you may need

34. FEEDING NEEDS OF YOUR TODDLER

With the progression from infancy to toddler, their dietary requirements too evolve. You will have to pack some snacks for travelling time. Fresh fruits and vegetables can be purchased at your destination. Most of the cities you travel to in whichever part of the world, will have baby food products and formulas, available at the local drug-store or the supermarket.

35. PICKING CLOTHES FOR YOUR BABY

Contrary to popular belief, babies can do without many changes of clothes. At the most pack 2 outfits per day. Pack mix and match type clothes for your little one as well. Pick things which are comfortable to wear and quick to dry.

36. SELECTING SHOES FOR YOUR BABY

Like outfits, kids can make do with two pairs of comfortable shoes. If you can get some water resistant shoes it will be best. To expedite drying wet shoes, you can stuff newspaper in them then wrap them with newspaper and leave them to dry overnight.

37. KEEP ONE CHANGE OF CLOTHES HANDY

Travelling with kids can be tricky. Keep a change of clothes for the kids and mum handy in your purse or tote bag. This takes a bit of space in your hand luggage but comes extremely handy in case there are any accidents or spills.

38. LEAVE BEHIND BABY ACCESSORIES

Baby accessories like their bed, bath tub, car seat, crib etc. should be left at home. Many hotels provide a crib on request, while car seats can be borrowed from friends or rented. Babies can be given a bath in the hotel sink or even in the adult bath tub with a little bit of water. If you bring a few bath toys, they can be used in the bath, pool, and out of water. They can also be sanitized easily in the sink.

39. CARRY A SMALL LOAD OF PLASTIC BAGS

With children around there are chances of a number of soiled clothes and diapers. These plastic bags help to sort the dirt from the clean inside your big bag.

>TOURIST

These are very light weight and come in handy to other carry stuff as well at times.

PACK WITH A PURPOSE

40. PACKING FOR BUSINESS TRIPS

One neutral-colored suit should suffice. It can be paired with different shirts, ties and accessories for different occasions. One pair of black suit pants could be worn with a matching jacket for the office or with a snazzy top for dinner.

41. PACKING FOR A CRUISE

Most cruises have formal dinners, and that formal dress usually takes up a lot of space. However you might find a tuxedo to rent. For women, a short black dress with multiple accessory options will do the trick.

42. PACKING FOR A LONG TRIP OVER DIFFERENT CLIMATES

The secret packing mantra for travel over multiple climates is layering. Layering traps air around your body creating insulation against the cold. The same light t-shirt that is comfortable in a warmer climate can be the innermost layer in a colder climate.

REDUCE SOME MORE WEIGHT

43. LEAVE PRECIOUS THINGS AT HOME

Things that you would hate to lose or get damaged leave them at home. Precious jewelry, expensive gadgets or dresses, could be anything. You will not require these on your trip. Leave them at home and spare the load on your mind.

44. SEND SOUVENIRS BY MAIL

If you have spent all your money on purchasing souvenirs, carrying them back in the same bag that you brought along would be difficult. Either pack everything in another bag and check it in the airport or get everything shipped to your home. Use an international carrier for a secure transit, but this could be more expensive than the checking fees at the airport.

45. AVOID CARRYING BOOKS

Books equal to weight. There are many reading apps which you can download on your smart phone or tab.

> TOURIST

Plus there are gadgets like Kindle and Nook that are thinner and lighter alternatives to your regular book.

CHECK, GET, SET, CHECK AGAIN

46. STRATEGIZE BEFORE PACKING

Create a travel list and prepare all that you think you need to carry along. Keep everything on your bed or floor before packing and then think through once again – do I really need that? Any item that meets this question can be avoided. Remove whatever you don't really need and pack the rest.

47. TEST YOUR LUGGAGE

Once you have fully packed for the trip take a test trip with your luggage. Take your bags and go to town for window shopping for an hour. If you enjoy your hour long trip it is good to go, if not, go home and reduce the load some more. Repeat this test till you hit the right weight.

48. ADD A ROLL OF DUCT TAPE

You might wonder why, when this book has been talking about reducing stuff, we're suddenly asking you to pack something totally unusual. This is because when you have limited supplies, duct tape is immensely helpful for small repairs – a broken bag, leaking zip-lock bag, broken sunglasses, you name it and duct tape can fix it, temporarily.

49. LIST OF ESSENTIAL ITEMS

Even though the emphasis is on packing light, there are things which have to be carried for any trip. Here is our list of essentials:

- Passport/Visa or any other ID

- Any other paper work that might be required on a trip like permits, hotel reservation confirmations etc.

- Medicines – all your prescription medicines and emergency kit, especially if you are travelling with children

- Medical or vaccination records

- Money in foreign currency if travelling to a different country

- Tickets- Email or Message them to your phone

\>TOURIST

50. MAKE THE MOST OF YOUR TRIP

Wherever you are going, whatever you hope to do we encourage you to embrace it whole-heartedly. Take in the scenery, the culture and above all, enjoy your time away from home.

On a long journey even a straw weighs heavy.

-Spanish Proverb

>TOURIST

PACKING AND PLANNING TIPS

A Week before Leaving

- Arrange for someone to take care of pets and water plants.
- Stop mail and newspaper.
- Notify Credit Card companies where you are going.
- Change your thermostat settings.
- Car inspected, oil is changed, and tires have the correct pressure.
- Passports and photo identification is up to date.
- Pay bills.
- Copy important items and download travel Apps.
- Start collecting small bills for tips.

Right Before Leaving

- Clean out refrigerator.
- Empty garbage cans.
- Lock windows.
- Make sure you have the proper identification with you.
- Bring cash for tips.
- Remember travel documents.
- Lock door behind you.
- Remember wallet.
- Unplug items in house and pack chargers.

>TOURIST

READ OTHER GREATER THAN A TOURIST BOOKS

Greater Than a Tourist San Miguel de Allende Guanajuato Mexico: 50 Travel Tips from a Local by Tom Peterson

Greater Than a Tourist – Lake George Area New York USA: 50 Travel Tips from a Local by Janine Hirschklau

Greater Than a Tourist – Monterey California United States: 50 Travel Tips from a Local by Katie Begley

Greater Than a Tourist – Chanai Crete Greece: 50 Travel Tips from a Local by Dimitra Papagrigoraki

Greater Than a Tourist – The Garden Route Western Cape Province South Africa: 50 Travel Tips from a Local by Li-Anne McGregor van Aardt

Greater Than a Tourist – Sevilla Andalusia Spain: 50 Travel Tips from a Local by Gabi Gazon

Greater Than a Tourist – Kota Bharu Kelantan Malaysia: 50 Travel Tips from a Local by Aditi Shukla

Children's Book: Charlie the Cavalier Travels the World by Lisa Rusczyk

>TOURIST

> TOURIST

Visit Greater Than a Tourist for Free Travel Tips
http://GreaterThanATourist.com

Sign up for the Greater Than a Tourist Newsletter for discount days, new books, and travel information:
http://eepurl.com/cxspyf

Follow us on Facebook for tips, images, and ideas:
https://www.facebook.com/GreaterThanATourist

Follow us on Pinterest for travel tips and ideas:
http://pinterest.com/GreaterThanATourist

Follow us on Instagram for beautiful travel images:
http://Instagram.com/GreaterThanATourist

>TOURIST

> TOURIST

Please leave your honest review of this book on Amazon and Goodreads. Please send your feedback to GreaterThanaTourist@gmail.com as we continue to improve the series. We appreciate your positive and constructive feedback. Thank you.

>TOURIST

METRIC CONVERSIONS

TEMPERATURE

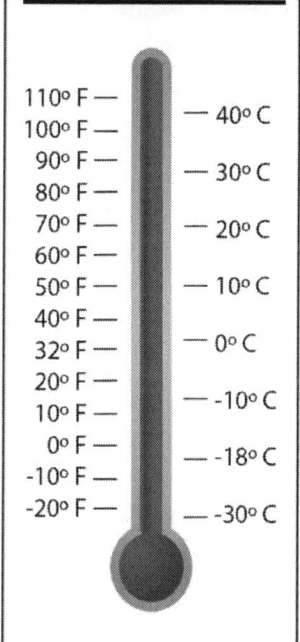

110° F — — 40° C
100° F —
90° F — — 30° C
80° F —
70° F — — 20° C
60° F —
50° F — — 10° C
40° F —
32° F — — 0° C
20° F —
10° F — — -10° C
0° F —
-10° F — — -18° C
-20° F —
— -30° C

To convert F to C:
Subtract 32, and then multiply by 5/9 or .5555.

To Convert C to F:
Multiply by 1.8 and then add 32.

32F = 0C

LIQUID VOLUME

To Convert:................Multiply by
U.S. Gallons to Liters.............. 3.8
U.S. Liters to Gallons 26
Imperial Gallons to U.S. Gallons 1.2
Imperial Gallons to Liters....... 4.55
Liters to Imperial Gallons 22

1 Liter = .26 U.S. Gallon
1 U.S. Gallon = 3.8 Liters

DISTANCE

To convert ....Multiply by
Inches to Centimeters 2.54
Centimeters to Inches 39
Feet to Meters...................... .3
Meters to Feet 3.28
Yards to Meters 91
Meters to Yards 1.09
Miles to Kilometers 1.61
Kilometers to Miles............ .62

1 Mile = 1.6 km
1 km = .62 Miles

WEIGHT

1 Ounce = .28 Grams
1 Pound = .4555 Kilograms
1 Gram = .04 Ounce
1 Kilogram = 2.2 Pounds

99

\>TOURIST

TRAVEL QUESTIONS

- Do you bring presents home to family or friends after a vacation?
- Do you get motion sick?
- Do you have a favorite billboard?
- Do you know what to do if there is a flat tire?
- Do you like a sun roof open?
- Do you like to eat in the car?
- Do you like to wear sun glasses in the car?
- Do you like toppings on your ice cream?
- Do you use public bathrooms?
- Did you bring your cell phone and does it have power?
- Do you have a form of identification with you?
- Have you ever been pulled over by a cop?
- Have you ever given money to a stranger on a road trip?
- Have you ever taken a road trip with animals?
- Have you ever went on a vacation alone?
- Have you ever run out of gas?

- If you could move to any place in the world, where would it be?
- If you could travel anywhere in the world, where would you travel?
- If you could travel in any vehicle, which one would it be?
- If you had three things to wish for from a magic genie, what would they be?
- If you have a driver's license, how many times did it take you to pass the test?
- What are you the most afraid of on vacation?
- What do you want to get away from the most when you are on vacation?
- What foods smells bad to you?
- What item do you bring on ever trip with you away from home?
- What makes you sleepy?
- What song would you love to hear on the radio when you're cruising on the highway?
- What travel job would you want the least?
- What will you miss most while you are away from home?
- What is something you always wanted to try?

>TOURIST

- What is the best road side attraction that you ever saw?
- What is the farthest distance you ever biked?
- What is the farthest distance you ever walked?
- What is the weirdest thing you needed to buy while on vacation?
- What is your favorite candy?
- What is your favorite color car?
- What is your favorite family vacation?
- What is your favorite food?
- What is your favorite gas station drink or food?
- What is your favorite license plate design?
- What is your favorite restaurant?
- What is your favorite smell?
- What is your favorite song?
- What is your favorite sound that nature makes?
- What is your favorite thing to bring home from a vacation?
- What is your favorite vacation with friends?
- What is your favorite way to relax?

- Where is the farthest place you ever traveled in a car?
- Where is the farthest place you ever went North, South, East and West?
- Where is your favorite place in the world?
- Who is your favorite singer?
- Who taught you how to drive?
- Who will you miss the most while you are away?
- Who if the first person you will contact when you get to your destination?
- Who brought you on your first vacation?
- Who likes to travel the most in your life?
- Would you rather be hot or cold?
- Would you rather drive above, below, or at the speed limited?
- Would you rather drive on a highway or a back road?
- Would you rather go on a train or a boat?
- Would you rather go to the beach or the woods?

>TOURIST

TRAVEL BUCKET LIST

1.

2.

3.

4.

5.

6.

7.

8.

9.

10.

>TOURIST

NOTES

Made in the USA
Middletown, DE
23 April 2021